OXFORD BOOK

Origin

The Big Game

PAUL SHIPTON

Starter (250 headwords)

Illustrated by Gavin Reece

Series Editor: Rachel Bladon
Founder Editors: Jennifer Bassett
and Tricia Hedge

OXFORD
UNIVERSITY PRESS

Great Clarendon Street, Oxford, OX2 6DP, United Kingdom

Oxford University Press is a department of the University of Oxford.
It furthers the University's objective of excellence in research, scholarship,
and education by publishing worldwide. Oxford is a registered trade
mark of Oxford University Press in the UK and in certain other countries

ISBN: 978 0 19 462448 0

A complete recording of this Bookworms edition of *The Big Game* is available.

Printed in China

Word count (main text): 1,316

For more information on the Oxford Bookworms Library,
visit www.oup.com/elt/gradedreaders

ACKNOWLEDGEMENTS

Cover photo: Getty Images (basketball game/Dmytro Aksonov)

Cover illustration by: Simon Reid

Illustrations by: Gavin Reece represented by Newdivision.co.uk

The publisher would like to thank the following for the permission to reproduce
photographs: 123RF p.32 (American Football match/Richard Kane); Alamy Stock Photo
pp.32 (Ultimate Frisbee match/Stephen Barnes/Sport), 42 (frisbee action shot/Stephen
Barnes/Sport); Getty Images p.31 (basketball game/Jason Miller); Oxford University
Press p.32 (volleyball match/Monkey Business Images); Shutterstock pp.32 (footballers/
Sooksun saksit), 32 (baseball game/zsolt_uveges), 32 (ice hockey match/Fotokvadrat).

CONTENTS

CHAPTER 1
The Worst Team?

"Good luck, Ben!" Emma calls to me before the game.

"Thanks," I say.

It's the first basketball game of the year for the West High School boys' team. There's one big question – can we do better than last year?

After one minute, we know the answer – no!

Our team is the worst team in town – we never win and everyone knows that.

When I get the ball, I see Jamie near the basket.

"Here, Ben!" he calls, so I throw the ball to him. He catches it and throws it at the basket.

It doesn't go in. The ball *never* goes in for Jamie.

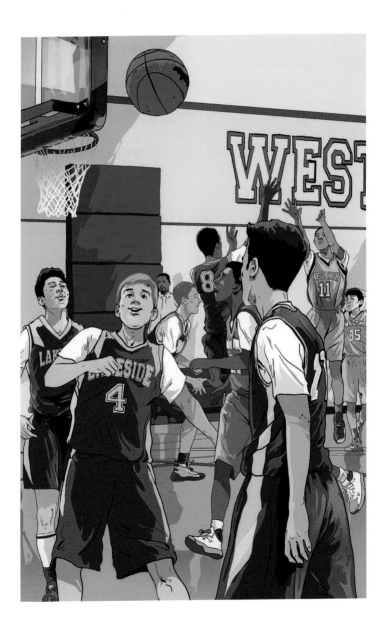

Of course, we lose – we *always* lose – but that's OK. We love playing.

Emma says, "Good game, Ben." I smile. She's the captain of the girls' basketball team at our school, and the girls' team is *good*.

A tall boy is watching us and he isn't smiling.

"Who's that?" I ask Emma, quietly.

"He's a new boy," she says. "He's in my class."

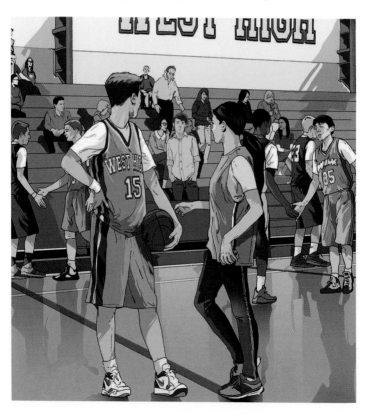

The tall boy comes and talks to me.

"Are you the captain?" he asks me. "I'm Sam. I'd like to be on the team."

"Can you play?" I ask.

Sam doesn't answer. He takes the ball from my hands and throws it. We aren't standing near the basket, but the ball goes in.

"Yes," says Sam quietly.

CHAPTER 2
Sam

After school the next day, our team meets in the gym. I bring Sam. "He's going to play on the team," I tell everyone.

At first, nobody is happy about this – do we *need* any new players?

So I throw the ball to Sam...

At once, everyone understands.

Sam is great – fast and strong. He can move past players easily. And when he throws the ball at the basket, he *always* scores.

I can't stop smiling. "What do you think?" I say to Jamie.

"Well…" says Jamie, "we aren't the worst team now."

CHAPTER 3
What a Player!

Before our next game, I see Emma again.

"Good luck!" she says.

"Thanks." I smile back at her. We don't need luck this time, I think.

No, everything is going to be different now. I can *feel* it.

We don't need all of our players because Sam is on the team now.

"Jamie, can you sit and watch today?" I ask.

"Oh… OK," says Jamie.

The game begins, and Sam is the best player there. He scores for our team again and again.

After the last break in the game, I say to Jamie, "Come and play for the last eight minutes." He smiles and runs to the team.

It's the last minute of the game. Sam has the ball, but there are two players in front of him. There's nobody near Jamie, so I shout, "Pass the ball to Jamie!"

Maybe Sam doesn't hear. He runs past the two players, then he jumps and throws.

Of course, he scores.

When the game ends, I run to the team. For the first time, we're the winners! Everyone is excited.

"Let's go to the coffee shop!" I say. After a game, we sometimes go to the coffee shop near school.

But Jamie is leaving. "I'm tired," he says. "I'm going home."

Emma looks at him, and at me. "I'm going home, too," she says.

Everything is different for our team now. We win the next game, and the game after that.

At school, people are excited. Everyone wants to watch us. I'm excited, too. And I'm *very* excited when I think about our next game. It's the game with East High School – the *big* game.

"How good *is* East High?" Sam asks me.

"Well, every player on their team is great," I tell him. "When we play games, East High always wins." I put my hand on Sam's arm. "But the players don't know about you…"

CHAPTER 4
The Big Day

The day of the big game is here, and I'm feeling excited.

I see Emma near the gym, but this time, she doesn't say, "Good luck!"

"Are you coming?" I ask.

"No. I'm not watching the game today," she says.

"What's the matter, Emma? You *always* watch us. And we're playing well now."

"No, *Sam* is playing well," Emma says.

"But we're winning games for the first time!" I say.

"One player wins for you, and you all stand and watch!" says Emma. "You want to win – I know that. But some things are more important. Sam is very good, but he never passes the ball. Ask Jamie – does *he* like having Sam on the team?"

I feel bad when Emma says this. She's right.

Just then, we hear a noise. Somebody is standing behind us – it's Sam.

"Sam, listen—" Emma begins to say, but Sam walks away.

"Come back!" I shout. "The game begins in ten minutes!"

"I can talk to him," Emma tells me. "But the team needs you *now*."

The team is waiting.

"Where's Sam?" Jamie asks.

"He... can't play today," I say.

"What? Then East High is going to *kill* us!"

"Maybe," I say, "but maybe not. Remember the most important thing – we're a *team*. So let's go and do our best!"

Jamie is afraid, I can see – but he's excited, too.

The game begins, and it isn't easy. The East High players are bigger, faster, stronger...

But everyone on our team runs for every ball now. We never stop working. We're a team again – I can see it. Maybe we can't win, but we can do our best.

Of course, East High is winning. The team has more points than us, but not many.

Seconds before the next break, I jump for the ball. East High's biggest player jumps, too, and hits me. I fall.

"Are you OK?" Jamie asks.

I stand slowly. "I... don't know. My leg is bad."

It's the break now. I'm happy because I can sit for five minutes. But can I play again with a bad leg?

Then I look up and see Emma and Sam.

CHAPTER 5
What a Team!

Sam doesn't want to be here, I can see.

"Ben, can you tell Sam something?" says Emma. "What's the most important thing for you in a game?"

That's easy.

"The team," I say. "You're a great player, Sam, but the team is the most important thing."

Emma smiles. "That's right," she says.

Sam is quiet. He's thinking.

I stand up – the game is starting again.

"Wait," says Emma. "What's wrong with your leg?"

"It isn't good," I say, "but the team needs me."

Sam looks at me. "That's all right, Ben," he says. "Sit down. I want to play... please."

When the game starts again, Sam is back with the team. I sit with Emma and watch.

Sam plays very well – of course – but he plays differently now. He doesn't take the ball all the time. He works with everyone and helps them.

"He's a team player now!" I say.

Emma smiles. "I know."

Soon, we're in the last minute of the game. East High has 24 points, and we have 24, too!

Sam has the ball. He isn't far from the basket, but there are lots of East High players near him.

"Come on, Sam!" I shout. "Score!"

But Sam passes the ball back… to Jamie!

Jamie catches the ball.

Two East High players are running at him. Jamie is afraid – I can see it – but he throws the ball...

It goes up, up, up. Everyone is quiet – they're all watching that ball.

And then...

… the ball goes into the basket in the last seconds of the game!

We're the winners!

I forget about my leg and jump up.

"What a game!" Emma says.

"Great, Jamie!" I say.

Everyone is happy, and I don't want the day to end.
"Come on, everyone – let's go to the coffee shop!" I say.

"Yes!" says Jamie happily. He smiles at our new team
player. "Are you coming, Sam?"

"Of course," Sam smiles, and we all leave. A team.

ball *(n)* a round thing for games like basketball and soccer

basket *(n)* Basketball players throw a ball into this when they score.

basketball *(n)* a game for two teams; players throw a ball into a basket

break *(n)* a short time when you stop working or playing

captain *(n)* the most important player in a team

catch *(v)* to take something (often a ball) in your hands

coffee shop *(n)* You can drink coffee here.

end *(v)* to stop

fall *(v)* to suddenly stop standing

game *(n)* something you play, like soccer or basketball

great *(adj)* very good

gym *(n)* a room or building for sports, e.g. basketball

jump *(v)* to move quickly up off the ground

maybe *(adv)* perhaps

pass *(v)* (in basketball) to throw the ball to somebody on your team

point *(n)* a mark (one, two, etc.) that you win in a game or sport

score *(v)* to win points in a game or sport

shout *(v)* to speak very loudly, because you are angry or want someone to hear you

start *(v)* to begin

strong *(adj)* You can move big and heavy things when you are strong.

team *(n)* people who play a sport (e.g. soccer) or game together

throw *(v)* to move your arm quickly and send something (e.g. a ball) through the air

win *(v)* to be the best or the first in a game or sport; **winner** *(n)*

Basketball

Basketball is a very popular sport. In the USA, lots of people like watching basketball, and it is the third most popular sport, after American football and baseball. But more people in the USA *play* basketball than any other team sport.

Number of players
Most basketball teams have twelve players, but only five people from a team can be on the basketball court at one time.

How to move the ball
You cannot run more than two steps with the ball in your hands. You can pass the ball to players on your team, or you can run and bounce the ball up and down.

How to score points
You throw the ball into the basket.

When you throw from here, you get 3 points.

When you throw from here, you get 2 points.

Famous teams and players

Some of the world's most famous basketball players play in the NBA (National Basketball Association) in the USA, for example LeBron James and Kobe Bryant. Famous NBA teams are the Chicago Bulls, the LA Lakers, and the Miami Heat.

LeBron James and Kobe Bryant

Did you know?

Many basketball players are very tall, but not *all* of them:

• NBA players Manute Bol and Gheorghe Mureşan: both 2.31 m!
• Mugsy Bogues: just 1.6 m!

RESEARCH & DISCUSS Read about basketball and then answer the questions.

1 Can you name two or three famous basketball players? Which teams do they play for?
2 Basketball is very popular in the USA. In which other countries is basketball very popular?

bounce *(v)* to make a ball go down and then back up
court *(n)* A basketball team plays here.
famous *(adj)* when lots of people know about someone or something
popular *(adj)* when lots of people like someone or something
sport *(n)* a game like soccer or basketball
step *(n)* when you move one foot in front of the other foot

Team Sports

American football (In the USA, people call this sport "football".)

soccer (In most countries, people call this "football".)

baseball

ice hockey

volleyball

ultimate

What sports do you like to play?

What sports do you like to watch?

The Big Game

ACTIVITIES

Think Ahead

1 Look at the back cover and the title. Which of these things are true? Write ✓ (yes) or ✗ (no).

1 The boys on the West High School basketball team are not happy because they often lose games. ☐

2 A new player, Sam, starts to play for the team. ☐

3 Sam is bad at basketball. ☐

4 The team starts to win games. ☐

2 **RESEARCH** Look at the team sports on page 32. Which of these sports are played at school in…

1 the USA?

2 the UK?

3 Australia?

3 **RESEARCH** What other sports are played at school in the countries in exercise 2?

Chapter Check

CHAPTER 1 Choose the correct words.

1 The West High School boys' basketball team is the *best* /
   worst team in town.

2 When Jamie throws the ball at the basket, it *always* /
   never goes in.

3 The girls' basketball team is *better* / *worse* than the
   boys' team.

4 The name of the team's captain is *Ben* / *Jamie*.

5 Sam wants to be *on the team* / *the team's captain*.

6 Sam is a *good* / *bad* basketball player.

CHAPTER 2 Are the sentences true or false?

1 The team meets in the gym before school.

2 When Ben says, "Sam is going to play on the team,"
   everyone is happy at first.

3 The players are thinking, "Do we need any new players?"
   but when Sam scores, they understand.

4 Sam doesn't often score.

5 Ben is not happy because Sam is on the the team now.

6 Jamie says, "We aren't the worst team now."

CHAPTER 3 Who says this to who?

Ben   Emma   Jamie   Sam   the team

1 "Good luck!"

_____ to _____

2 "Come and play for the last eight minutes."

_____ to _____

3 "Pass the ball to Jamie!"

_____ to _____

4 "Let's go to the coffee shop!"

_____ to _____

5 "I'm tired."

_____ to _____

6 "How good *is* East High?"

_____ to _____

CHAPTER 4 Put sentences a–g in the correct order.

a Sam hears Emma and Ben, and walks away.

b Ben tells the players, "Remember the most important thing – we're a *team*."

c Emma and Ben talk about the team.

d Ben sees Emma and Sam.

e The game begins without Sam.

f Ben is happy because there is a break.

g An East High School player hits Ben when he jumps for the ball.

CHAPTER 5 Match the sentence halves.

1　At first, Sam doesn't want...

2　Ben stands up because...

3　Sam wants Ben...

4　Emma and Ben are happy because...

5　There are lots of East High players near Sam, so...

6　Jamie is afraid, but...

7　When West High win the game, Ben forgets about his leg and...

8　After the game, the West High team

a　Sam is playing differently now.

b　he throws the ball and scores.

c　the game is starting again.

d　jumps up.

e　to be at the gym.

f　he passes the ball to Jamie.

g　all go to the coffee shop.

h　to sit down.

Focus on Vocabulary

1 Complete the text with the words.

captain   catches   pass   scores   team   throws   winners

The basketball game

Everyone on our ¹_____ plays well in the game.
I get the ball and I ²_____ it to Emma. She's our
team's ³_____. She ⁴_____ the ball and runs
past two players.

   Then she ⁵_____ the ball at the basket. She
⁶_____! We are the ⁷_____!

2 Match the words to the definitions.

break   coffee shop   gym   school   shout   strong

1 You do this when somebody can't hear you at first.

2 You can find students and teachers here.

3 You can buy a hot drink here.

4 Someone with big arms is often this.

5 You can play different sports or games in here.

6 You can stop working at this time.

Focus on Language

1 Add -*ly* or -*ily* to each word and complete the sentences.

1 Sam can run _____ (quick) with the ball.

2 "We're the winners!" Ben says _____ (happy).

3 The game starts and Sam plays _____ (different).

4 "I'd like to be on the team," Sam says _____ (quiet).

5 "I'm going home," says Jamie _____ (angry).

2 DECODE Read this text from the story. Look at the pronouns 1–5. Who or what do they describe? Choose the correct answers.

When ¹I get the ball, I see Jamie near the basket.
"Here, Ben!" ²he calls, so I throw the ball to ³him.
He catches ⁴it and throws ⁵it at the basket.

1 a Ben   b Jamie
2 a Ben   b Jamie
3 a Ben   b Jamie
4 a the ball   b the basket
5 a the ball   b the basket

Now write the correct pronoun for each name/word.

(The ball) _____ goes into the basket, and (Jamie) _____ jumps up happily.

Discussion

1 Read the dialogue. Complete the sentences.

MEGAN: In the story, Emma says, "Some things are more important than winning." I don't think that she's right. What do you think?

GEORGE: Winning is <u>important</u>, but what about doing your best in a game? I think that is the most important thing. Rosa, do you agree?

ROSA: I don't agree. For me, having a good time with friends is more important than winning or doing your best.

MEGAN: I think that they are all important. And I think that playing as a team is <u>very important</u>, too. But winning is more important.

1 _____ thinks that doing your best is the most important thing.

2 _____ thinks that having a good time with friends is more important than winning.

3 _____ thinks that winning is the most important thing.

4 _____ thinks that doing your best in a game, having a good time with friends, and playing as a team are all important.

2 Read the dialogue again and complete the phrases.

   1 What do you _____? / Do you _____? /
      But what _____...?

   2 I _____ agree. / I agree.

   3 For _____... / I _____ that...

3 Which of the phrases in exercise 2 are used for:

   a giving your opinion? _____

   b asking a question? _____

   c agreeing or disagreeing? _____

4 Look at the dialogue in exercise 1 again. Put the
   underlined words in the right place on the line below.

      ●————————●————————————●————————●

   the most important   not important

5 Say which of these things you think is (1) the most
   important; (2) very important; (3) important; (4) not
   important in a game.

   • winning

   • playing as a team

   • learning more so you can play better

   • having a good time with friends

6 Find someone else who has different answers from you.
   Discuss your answers using the phrases from exercise 2.

1 Read the poster about the team sport "ultimate." Would you like to play ultimate? Why/Why not?

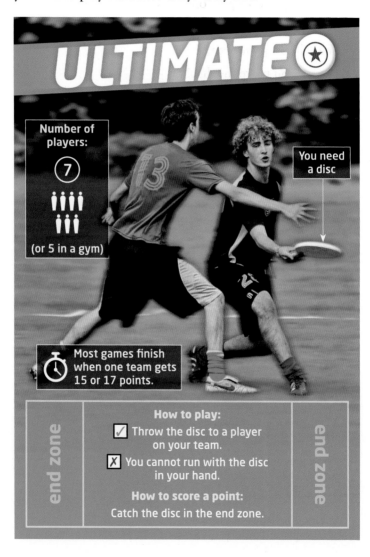

ULTIMATE ⊛

Number of players:

⑦

(or 5 in a gym)

You need a disc

Most games finish when one team gets 15 or 17 points.

end zone

How to play:
✓ Throw the disc to a player on your team.
✗ You cannot run with the disc in your hand.

How to score a point:
Catch the disc in the end zone.

end zone

2 Answer the questions about ultimate.

1 How many people play on a team?

2 What do you need to play?

3 When does a game end?

4 How do you move the disc?

5 What *can't* you do with the disc?

6 How do you score a point?

3 READ & RESEARCH Choose a different team sport. Research the sport.

Sport: soccer

Number of people on a team: 11

You need: a football

How long? 90 minutes

How to score? ...

4 CREATE Make a poster about the sport in exercise 3.

5 Ask other students about their sports. (You can use the questions in exercise 2.)

6 Which sport would you most like to play? Why?

If you liked this Bookworm, why not try...

Sing to Win

STARTER
Andrea Sarto

Sing to Win is the biggest programme on TV – everyone watches it and every singer wants to win it. Sofia loves singing, so she goes to an audition for *Sing to Win* – and makes friends with Emma. Emma is a very good singer, too, and soon there are stories about the two friends on TV and online. But not all the stories are true – and suddenly, being friends is not easy...

Nobody Listens

STAGE 1
Rowena Wakefield

Alex's family are always moving from town to town. He doesn't make new friends now, because he doesn't like saying goodbye to them. He has his music, his songs, and his guitar, and they're only for him. It's best like that, he thinks.

Then he meets Bella, and everything gets difficult. He likes her. He likes her very much. But she wants him to play his music for everyone. And how can he say goodbye to her, when his parents decide to move again?
